The World of
WHALES, DOLPHINS & PORPOISES

Printed in China

03 04 05 06 07 5 4 3 2 1

Library of Congress Cataloging-in-Publication Data

Martin, Tony, 1954—
The World of whales, dolphins & porpoises / Tony Martin.
p. cm.
Includes bibliographical references (p 96).
ISBN 0-89658-579-4 (hardcover)
1. Cetacea I. Title: World of whales, dolphins, and porpoises.
II. Title.
QL737.C4 M3144 2003
599.5—dc21

2002151889

Distributed in Canada by Raincoast Books, 9050 Shaughnessy Street, Vancouver, B.C. V6P 6E5

Published by Voyageur Press, Inc.
123 North Second Street, P.O. Box 338, Stillwater, MN 55082 U.S.A.
651-430-2210, fax 651-430-2211
books@voyageurpress.com   www.voyageurpress.com

Educators, fundraisers, premium and gift buyers, publicists, and marketing managers:
Looking for creative products and new sales ideas? Voyageur Press books are available at special discounts when purchased in quantities,
and special editions can be created to your specifications. For details contact the marketing department at 800-888-9653.

The World of
WHALES, DOLPHINS & PORPOISES

Tony Martin

Voyageur Press

Contents

Whales, Dolphins and Porpoises

An Arctic shoreline in late summer. A polar bear ambles gracefully along the shingle beach. The ice-strewn sea is flat calm. Walruses periodically bob to the surface in their own comical way, a permanent look of surprise on their faces. I'm puttering gently along the coast of Wrangel Island in eastern Siberia in a Zodiac inflatable boat, just far enough out from the tide-line to prevent my propeller pinging the boulders dotting these shallow waters. Ahead is a small group of Arctic terns, wheeling and hovering noisily over a small spot of water. Knowing that this can herald something interesting, I stop the engine and slide up to the focus of interest. Nothing. A minute, two minutes later, still nothing. I'm about to start the engine again, when a large swirl of water rises to the surface and encircles the little boat. I'm puzzled; no currents, no nearby walruses, no obvious big rocks. Then, a boat-length ahead, a small dark triangle pierces the surface and disappears. Strange. Almost immediately, and a boat-length behind, a smooth rounded flipper-like object rises above the water, wafts in a semi-circle and disappears. Stranger still, but surely not, not HERE! As my brain finally put the pieces together, the adult gray whale turns right-way-up, raises its barnacle-encrusted head to blow (reminding me in the process that their breath smells *really* bad) and slides out from directly underneath the Zodiac in one powerful thrust of its tail. And then, before my heart has stopped thumping, a second one follows.

These two monsters, shortly before starting a migration which would take them from the frigid Russian Arctic to the sub-tropical heat of Mexico, had clearly been feeding in the mud less than a stone's throw from the beach and in water so shallow that they were probably resting on their sides. Indeed, they swam in a circle to resume their supper a few hundred meters away. Not terminally ill and in the process of stranding, as was my first guess, these animals were perfectly healthy and no doubt doing what gray whales have been doing along these shores for centuries.

Mulling over the day's events later that evening, it struck me how, even after nearly a quarter of a century of research fieldwork with whales, something catches me by surprise nearly every trip. In truth, I and my biologist colleagues around the world are barely scratching the surface of knowledge about this fascinating group of animals. There is much to learn.

So this book cannot claim to reveal everything about whales, dolphins and porpoises, because they retain too many secrets. What it will do, I hope, using a combination of up-to-date information and beautiful photographs, is inform, explain, excite and inspire in equal measure. As you turn the last page I trust that you, too, will share the sense of awe and wonder which is undiminished in me, 25 years after discovering at first hand that whales have bad breath.

Gray whales can be closely approached and show little fear of man, perhaps because they have been protected for decades. During the whaling era, mothers were known as 'devil fish' because they aggressively defended their calves.

What is a Whale?

Whales, dolphins and porpoises, known collectively as cetaceans (from the taxonomic Order of mammals to which they belong – the *Cetacea*) come in a bewildering range of shapes and sizes. Everyone knows the largest, because it also happens to be the largest creature ever to have lived on Earth – the blue whale (*Balaenoptera musculus*). But it may come as a surprise that animals with a body weight only one three-thousandth that of a blue whale (porpoises and some dolphins) have many features and the same evolutionary origins in common. Those origins are also shared by ungulates (even-toed animals like deer, sheep and hippos), the ancestors of both groups being condylarths – furred land predators which lived in the region of the ancient Tethys Sea. Over millions of years, a branch of the condylarths and their descendants adopted an increasingly aquatic existence, eventually evolving physical characteristics which made living in water easier. These included the development of a horizontal tail for propulsion, the reduction of hind limbs, and the gradual migration of nostrils from the front of the head towards the top. Some 45-50 million years ago, the first recognizably whale-like creatures, called archaeocetes, were an established part of the ancient marine ecosystem. The archaeocetes evolved and diversified, and were in turn succeeded by creatures very similar to those we know today.

The similar body form shared by all modern cetaceans masks the fact that two fundamentally different groups of animals are included under the same umbrella name. Most of the largest whales are filter feeders, without teeth, and known as baleen whales or Mysticetes (from the taxonomic sub-Order name *Mysticeti*). The remaining whales, and all the dolphins and porpoises, have teeth and form the sub-Order *Odontoceti*, with the collective name toothed whales or Odontocetes. Current evidence suggests that the two lineages probably developed during the Oligocene (26-38 million years ago).

Baleen whales strain dense swarms of very small creatures called zooplankton from the water, and sometimes schools of fish. Baleen is the name given to the filtering apparatus which has replaced teeth in the Mysticetes. It takes the form of closely packed, triangular plates which hang from the roof of the mouth, one row on each side. The inner edge of each plate has a fringe of fibers which combine to form a dense mat lining the inside of the mouth. Food-laden water passes in through the open mouth and out through the baleen, leaving the food organisms trapped on the fibers. A large sub-group of baleen whales known as rorquals are distinguished by expanding pleats in the elastic tissue of the throat and thorax, known as ventral grooves, which allow these animals to engulf tons of food-laden seawater in a single mouthful. The water is then forced out through the baleen, leaving the prey – usually krill or small fish – to be licked off and swallowed.

Toothed whales, or Odontocetes, feed very differently, in that they generally catch prey items individually. Nevertheless, a number of different feeding strategies are pursued across this group of animals, not least because the

The humpback whale is one of the most recognizable of all cetaceans, and famous for its haunting song. This whale is breaching – a behavior that is often repeated many times in quick succession and is a form of display. The lines on the throat of this animal are known as ventral grooves. They allow the tissue to expand like pleated fabric as the whale engulfs huge quantities of water during feeding.

shape of the mouth and number and shape of teeth varies greatly. At one extreme are the species with forceps-like jaws and literally dozens of sharp teeth designed for grasping prey. At the other are the beaked whales and narwhal with few, if any, functional teeth. Even in this strange company, the male strap-toothed whale is in a league of its own; the only teeth *it* has eventually grow over the upper jaw and prevent the mouth from opening more than a few inches/centimeters!

The exact number of different cetacean species with which we share this planet is open to question. The reason is simply lack of knowledge. New species are being discovered even as we begin the twenty-first century, and even a long-established 'species' like the minke whale we now know to be an artificial grouping of two (or perhaps more) similar-looking species. This process of scientific discovery and re-evaluation will continue as new research tools become available. In particular, the ever-developing field of genetic analysis is producing some extraordinary surprises, shaking to its core the purely descriptive basis on which taxonomy previously relied. The number of cetacean species recognized at the time of publication of this book is 85, of which 14 are baleen whales and 71 are toothed whales (including dolphins and porpoises). It would not be surprising if this number crept up to 90 within a decade; not because any new species will evolve in that time, but because our ability to recognize species for what they are is always improving.

The English names 'whale', 'dolphin' and 'porpoise' broadly reflect body size in decreasing order, but can be confusing. For example, the killer whale and the two pilot whales are actually large examples of the family Delphinidae – the marine dolphins. Furthermore, some species are known by two or more names even in the English language; beluga or white whale, killer whale or orca, for example. Even scientific names change as taxonomists revise the classification of this group of animals. The dolphin which lives in the river Indus was known until recently as *Platanista minor*, but is now called *Platanista gangetica*. The dolphin hasn't suddenly changed; we've changed our minds about what to call it!

Form and Function

Despite the great variety of body size, shape and marking we see in cetaceans, some features are common to them all and collectively distinguish them from all other creatures. The overall body shape, for example, is torpedo-like; long, smooth and (with the glorious exception of the male narwhal) stripped of projections which might increase hydrodynamic drag. The forelimbs are streamlined, and the hind limbs are now represented only by vestigial bones hidden in the abdomen. The tail and dorsal fin are shaped like aircraft wings in cross-section – rounded on the leading edge and tapered to nothing on the trailing edge – again to minimize drag. The tail itself is horizontal, in contrast to fish, and consists of dense fibrous tissue attached to the end of the spine. It is powered by formidable muscles which lie alongside the spine and dominate the upper half of cetaceans from the fin rearwards, power being delivered mostly on the up-stroke as the muscles contract. In most cetaceans the tail is divided along the mid-line into two symmetrical halves, known as flukes, with a notch between them on the trailing edge. For the great majority of species which possess a dorsal fin, this appendage provides rotational stability much like the tail fin on an aircraft. This fin reaches its greatest development in male killer whales, and is so abnormally large in this animal that it must surely serve another purpose – probably that of sexual advertisement.

The sleek cetacean profile owes much to the thick layer of blubber which covers the entire body like a cocoon. This tissue has three key functions. It reduces drag by smoothing what would otherwise be a more angular body shape, acts as an energy reservoir by storing fat, and provides a critical insulating barrier between a core body temperature of 98°F (36.7°C) and a surrounding water temperature which is near 32°F (0°) for some species of whale. Streamlining is further improved by virtue of the reproductive organs being held within the body cavity, rather than (as in most land mammals) hanging externally. An udder like a cow's, or a scrotum like a bull's would be a severe impediment to rapid swimming, especially when you consider that the combined weight of a right whale's testicles can be more than a ton!

We learn as children that mammals are supposed to have hair, yet none is obvious on dolphins or whales when we see them swimming. In fact, very sparse hair can be found on the head of the fetus (unborn young) of many species, the juveniles of some and on adults of a few. The large pimples on the forward part of the humpback whale head are hair follicles, and the elongate jaws of the Amazon river dolphin have noticeable bristles. In general, though, cetaceans are effectively hairless.

Perhaps the greatest burden to a mammal living in water is the need to gather oxygen, actually to *exchange* old lung gases for new, at the surface. The uppermost part of the water column is where predators lurk, and where there is often little food, so time here should be minimized. This has resulted in several physiological adaptations in cetaceans, the most obvious of which is that the nostrils are positioned on the top of the head so that a breath can be taken without

During high-speed travel, marine dolphins often leap clear of the water to breathe. This bottlenose dolphin shows the classical, streamlined body shape that allows rapid movement through water. The swept-back dorsal fin provides stability, but not all dolphins possess one.

needing to pause forward motion. Time at the surface is further reduced by means of the explosive 'blow' and immediate inhalation. Most of the lung volume is emptied and refilled very rapidly like this; dolphins do so in the blink of an eye. Anyone who has been very close to a large whale when it blows can attest to the pressure of air being expelled, the noisy blast being particularly unnerving if the animal rises unexpectedly behind you in a small boat.

The external adaptation to air breathing is matched by internal modifications which extend the amount of time a cetacean can hold its breath. These physiological changes allow the animal to load its body with much more oxygen than the lungs alone could hold. An important reason for this in deep-diving species is that the lungs collapse under water pressure long before the animals reach depths at which they normally forage. Despite this, a sperm whale or beaked whale can remain submerged for an hour or more, and it does so mainly using oxygen stored chemically in the blood and muscles. Other physiological processes further extend the length of time the animal can stay away from the surface, such as the shutting down of non-essential oxygen burning functions like digestion. The depth to which a whale or dolphin dives depends mostly on how long it can hold its breath. Even the smallest species can dive below the depth at which the lungs collapse, and the animal itself (being mostly water) is incompressible. Consequently, a dive to 3300 ft (1000 m), where the pressure is well over half a ton per square inch (500 kg to 6.5 sq cm), is little different to one reaching 660 ft (200 m) except for the time needed to descend and ascend. Generally speaking, larger Odontocetes dive for longer and dive deeper than smaller ones. But the baleen whales, despite being very big, are rather poor performers in this regard. A small toothed whale like the beluga routinely dives much deeper than does a blue whale, for example.

A question commonly asked is why whales do not suffer from 'the bends' and High Pressure Nervous Syndrome, afflictions in man which can result in the injury or death of a diver. The answer is that cetaceans have yet more physiological mechanisms which prevent such problems. These include a network of tiny blood vessels known as the *rete mirabile* (miraculous net) which filter gas bubbles from the blood before they can cause trouble in the brain or other tissues, and they can tolerate nitrogen concentrations in muscle which could kill a man. Another crucial difference between cetaceans and human divers is that we continue to breathe pressurized air from tanks on our backs while under the surface, whereas of course whales and dolphins carry only one 'lungful' of air on a dive.

Distribution and Migration

Most cetaceans are marine creatures, and could theoretically swim to all corners of the Earth's oceans and seas. But they do not. Why? Why does the harbor porpoise, so widespread along the coasts of the North Atlantic and North Pacific Oceans, not occur in the middle of these great bodies of water? And why is it not found in the South Atlantic or South Pacific? Why is the killer whale familiar to people venturing to high latitudes in both the Arctic and Antarctic, and many places in between, yet the vaquita is unknown outside a tiny finger of sea in western Mexico? The answers to these questions are often complex, and involve the realization that the distributional patterns of cetaceans, as with most animals, are in a continual process of change. What we see today is different from the situation existing even a few thousand years ago, a blink of an evolutionary eye, let alone a million years. Similarly, things will look different again a thousand years from now.

The fact is that sea mammal distribution is shaped by barriers. These barriers may be very solid, like the coastline of a continent, or they may be as invisible to us as the edge of a current or the cusp of an underwater shelf. The geographical limit of some cetaceans is the result of an influence which has long since disappeared. The strange pattern of the long-finned pilot whale is a case in point. This cool-water species currently occurs widely in the Southern Ocean, but has a substantial outpost in the North Atlantic, the two populations now separated by thousands of miles of

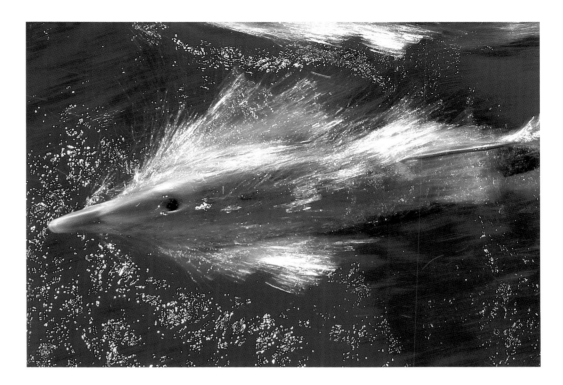

tropical waters. The most likely explanation for this split distribution is that animals crossed the equator during an earlier period of global cooling and were subsequently cut off from the main group when temperatures subsequently increased again, rendering the Equatorial region inhospitable.

Although individual species may have strong preferences for, say, shallow water, or a narrow temperature band, cetaceans as a whole have adapted to an extraordinarily wide range of habitats. Collectively, they cover almost all waters around the globe. My own field experience demonstrates this well. I have spent 12 years exploring the lifestyle of the beluga, an Arctic animal which

The near effortless movement of cetaceans allows them to cover vast distances at little cost.

This right whale tail (opposite) will propel its owner many thousands of miles during each migrational cycle.

Unlike most dolphins, the diminutive tucuxi (above) has populations in both marine and fresh waters.

A pod of female belugas on migration (opposite), some with young calves.

environments, yet both are 'home' to cetaceans – the most widely distributed Order of mammals on the planet.

Another difference between the beluga and the boto (also known as the Amazon river dolphin) is that the latter remains year-round in the same geographical area, whereas belugas alternate between summer and winter grounds in sequence with the cyclical pattern of Arctic sea-ice. This seasonal movement from one area to another is a classic example of migration. Cetacean migrations vary in scale from less than 125 mi (200 km) in the case of belugas in the St Lawrence river, Canada, up to many thousands of mi/km in most baleen whales. One of the best-known baleen whale migrations is that of the humpback whale which, like many other similar species, moves from food-rich cold waters in summer to warmer but unproductive areas in winter. The reason for this long swim is reproduction – calves are born, and mating takes place, in the tropical waters of places like the Caribbean and Hawaii. But the cost is high because these animals have to go without significant food for periods of several months. They prepare for this by fattening up in the summer months, converting dense clouds of zooplankton and fish into fat which is deposited in their blubber layer and subsequently burned up slowly during the breeding season. Pregnant females must begin the winter in especially good condition because they need to nourish the fetus growing within them, and after its birth will need to find energy both for themselves and for the huge quantities of fat-rich milk that the youngster requires if it is to survive.

took my breath away as I followed the tracks of radio-tagged whales on a computer screen. They merrily swam into frigid areas which were literally covered in sea ice, and which by any normal logic should be fatal to a creature which needs to breathe at the water surface. In total contrast, I am writing these words on a tethered raft in the Brazilian Amazon, with dense tropical forest on all sides and two species of dolphin (boto and tucuxi) swimming beneath me. The water is fresh, warm and turbid from the sediment it carries between the Andes and this great river's mouth at the Atlantic, some 1500 mi (2500 km) away. It would be difficult to imagine a greater contrast between these two

Life History

Like all mammals, whales, dolphins and porpoises mate, give birth to live young and suckle the calf. Unlike all other mammals except Sirenians (manatees and dugong), however, they have to do all this under water. Even seals carry out most of their reproductive activities on land or ice.

The cetacean reproductive cycle is not very different from our own, in that pregnancy lasts a little less than a year in most species, and the nursing period varies from around eight months to two or more years. Mating is not often observed, but we know that activity peaks at a particular time of year in most species, because births are usually concentrated into a period of a few months. Marine dolphins enjoy a very active sex life, and right whales are flagrantly sexual, with several males jostling for access to receptive females. The females can retain control of the situation, and be selective, by the simple expediency of lying upside down at the surface, their underside exposed only to the air. The obvious promiscuity of both sexes, and the enormous size of a right whale's testes and penis, strongly indicates that sperm competition operates in these animals, i.e. that the father of the single calf is most likely to be the mating partner which inseminated the most vigorous, and greatest number, of sperm. Promiscuity is probably the most common mating system in cetaceans, and none are thought to form monogamous pair bonds as are seen in swans, albatrosses and many human societies, for example. In no cetacean species are males known to provide any help or protection specifically to the female(s) with which they mated, or to their own calves; indeed it is unlikely that any cetacean father could recognize its own offspring. Any benefit a mate or father might provide would be through the defense or leadership of a group in which there may be many relatives, and even this will be restricted to the social Odontocetes (toothed whales, dolphins and porpoises), i.e. those that live in stable groups.

Pregnancy is completed in about 10 months in porpoises, about 11 months in baleen whales and up to 15 months in killer whales and sperm whales. Ironically, a huge blue whale calf (born at around 5500 lb (2500 kg) takes much less time to develop than a beluga calf, which enters the world at only 175 lb (80 kg). A single calf is always born. Twin fetuses occur very rarely, but no example of a successful multiple whale or dolphin birth has ever been recorded. Birth is normally tail-first in dolphins and is probably head-first in baleen whales, though exceptionally few births of wild cetaceans have been witnessed by man. Immediately after delivery into the sea, the calf is helped to the surface for its first breath by the mother. The two then retain a very close bond for the first few months after birth. During this time the youngster learns first to suckle without swallowing mouthfuls of water (the mother helps by squirting milk from the nipple), then how to catch live prey.

Maternal care and lactation are completed in less than a year in many baleen whales and some porpoise populations, but last longer than a year in most dolphins and all the larger toothed whales. Baleen whale calves, in particular, grow at a

Humpback whale calves grow extremely fast on a diet of rich milk, and follow their mothers thousands of miles on migration during the first months of life. They are usually weaned before their first birthday, allowing the female to devote her resources to a new pregnancy.

Bottlenose dolphins (above) remain with their mothers for many years.

Gray whale calves (opposite) are born in warm, protected lagoons along the Baja peninsula of Mexico.

phenomenal rate on a diet of very fatty milk (often more than 30 per cent fat) produced in prodigious quantities by their mothers. In the case of the social marine dolphins and whales, female calves often remain in their mothers' social group for their entire lives, though males probably leave to join other groups before adulthood. Even so, mothers may continue to provide supplementary milk to calves for many years; there are examples of five-year-old and even ten-year-old animals still suckling.

Having weaned, the young cetacean spends time growing, and developing its survival and social skills before reaching the age at which it, too, will start reproducing. This period of adolescence can be as short as a year or two in the harbor porpoise, or as long as 20 or more years in the bowhead whale. In general, females become sexually mature before males, particularly in those species like the sperm whale where adult males are larger than adult females. Here, the largest bulls are the most successful, and they may fight other bulls for supremacy and access to females, so smaller and younger males have few mating chances. After their first calf, females may give birth again a year later (some harbor porpoises and minke whales), two years later (most rorquals) or, more usually, they wait three or more years before producing another calf. The intervening time is taken up with providing milk to the calf, a rest period, and a year or so of the new pregnancy. It is unusual for cetaceans to conceive while lactating, probably because of the large amount of energy required to grow a fetus and produce milk simultaneously. But some harbor porpoise and minke whale populations do this routinely, suggesting that they can find plenty of food.

As in most animal groups, the cetaceans which begin reproduction early in life, and produce offspring in quick succession, live relatively short lives. Those that live life in the slow lane tend to live longest. Good examples of both ends of the spectrum are the harbor porpoise mentioned above and bowhead whale; these porpoises rarely reach 15 years of age, yet bowhead whales often live to more than 100 years. Despite this enormous difference in longevity, average females of the two species probably produce a similar number of offspring during their lives.

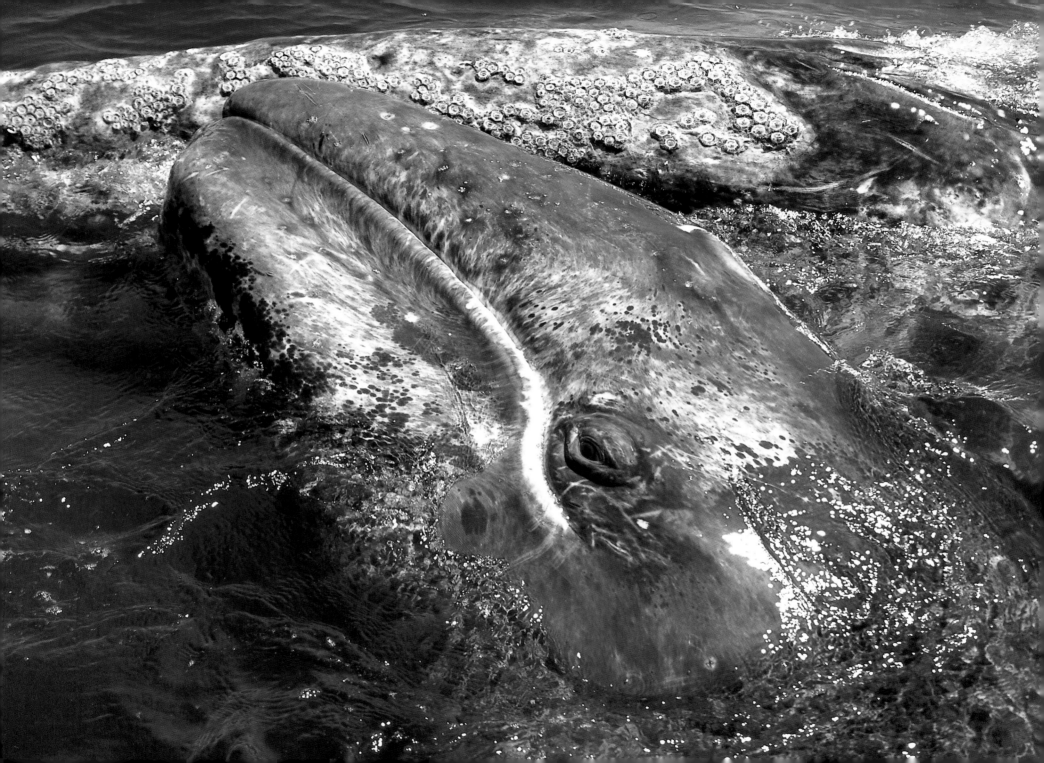

With the mountains of Kaikoura, New Zealand, in the background this
bull sperm whale is in one of the best-known whale hot spots in the world.

Senses

In the same way that living in a dense medium like water has profound effects on the way cetaceans look and move, so it does too on the way they sense the world around them. We, and most other air-living mammals, use light as the primary means of gathering environmental information. How fast is that car moving? How near is the mountain we aim to climb? Who is that person on the other side of the street? But light is poorly transmitted in all but the clearest water, and barely at all in the depths to which many cetaceans dive, so whales and dolphins mostly use sound – which carries fast in water – as an alternative source of information. In most situations baleen whales manage, we think, by interpreting sound which is produced elsewhere; the acoustic equivalent of you or me going out at night and relying on starlight, streetlights and other people's flashlights to tell us where we are and what is going on around us. In contrast, dolphins and toothed whales – the Odontocetes – use their own acoustic flashlights, produce their own sound, to provide more detailed information about their immediate surroundings. This sound production is

accompanied by sensitive and sophisticated sound reception abilities which allow an animal to interpret echoes at a mind-boggling rate, the pulses sounding like a buzz to our ears. The result is a sense so acute that dolphins can chase and catch small, fast-swimming fish, following their twists and turns with great accuracy right up to the point where they are picked off. This can be done even in total darkness or, as in the case of the Indian river dolphin, when effectively blind. Amazing

Diving for fish, a dolphin uses echolocation clicks in the same way that a bat searches for flying insects.

though this ability, known as echolocation, certainly is, it is not confined to large-brained dolphins. We are all familiar with it as a characteristic of bats, in which it evolved independently and in the much less dense medium of air.

It is still not clear exactly how cetaceans make echolocation 'clicks', but there is no doubt that the sounds leave the head through an organ known as the 'melon'. This soft, rounded tissue sits on the rostrum (flat part of the head) of toothed whales and forms what we might call the forehead of the animal. The shape of the melon can be visibly changed at will by some species like the beluga and boto, and acts as an acoustic lens, focusing sound at different distances from the head.

Although sight is of secondary importance to the Odontocetes, if not all cetaceans, it is still a significant means of gathering information at and near the surface where light penetrates. The eyes are always positioned on the side of the head, giving binocular vision ahead and below in most species, but not to the sides. Cetacean eyes have an iris which adjusts to varying levels of light, but in other ways their eyes are less sophisticated than our own. For example, recent research has shown that they have lost the ability to detect color, and many species may have eyes which are permanently focused at infinity. One species, the Indian river dolphin, has no eye lens at all, and its tiny eyes may be good for little more than

A humpback whale rises to 'spyhop' –
to take a look at the world above the water surface.
The bulbous foreheads of these pilot whales (opposite) comprise
an organ called a 'melon' that focuses their echolocation clicks.

telling light from dark. These deficiencies are adaptations to changed circumstances. The remote ancestors of today's cetaceans almost certainly had eyes that had evolved for use in clear air, not murky water, and water-living animals have different needs.

The sense of touch is well developed in cetaceans, as evidenced by the level of tactile contact social dolphins exhibit. The sensitivity of their skin is variable, being particularly acute around the mouth, blowhole, genital area and flippers. Another sense, taste, is certainly used in sensing water-borne chemicals, and must play a role in sexual and social signaling by detecting and interpreting body secretions. Captive dolphins sometimes show food preferences, and this may also be linked with taste. The small olfactory sensors in baleen whales indicate that smell is almost certainly not a key element in their lives, and as yet there is no evidence that it is used at all in Odontocetes. Taste and smell are therefore probably less acute in cetaceans than in humans.

We should also consider here what we might call the cetacean's sense of direction – the ability to navigate in what you or I would see only as a featureless ocean. The types of experiment which have shown how birds navigate are much less easy with something the size of a whale, and consequently much less is known about cetaceans in this regard than many other animals. It is clear, though, that cetaceans of many species routinely carry out migrations which must require the use of one or more navigational sense, the most likely being those that use sound, the Earth's magnetism, and the stars. The ability to use celestial navigation has been proven in even small birds, so it is entirely plausible that cetaceans use it too. Sound

Dolphins are tactile animals, often gently touching each other with body and fins.

The blows of four humpback whales (opposite) are backlit in the sheltered waters of southern Alaska.

There is some evidence that a magnetic sense, found in birds and land mammals (even ourselves), is very likely also used by cetaceans. The physical evidence is the finding of traces of magnetite, a mineral ore sensitive to magnetism, in the bone tissue surrounding the brain of some whales. We don't know how, or even if, this substance is used, but its presence is at least indicative of some magnetic sense in these animals. The behavioral evidence is that mass strandings of cetaceans in Britain, the beaching of often tens or hundreds of apparently healthy animals, seem to be linked to sites of magnetic anomaly. This theory has not been supported by research elsewhere, but at face value seems appealing. It would account for the fact that re-floated whales often turn around

Rescuers work to save a stranded pod of false killer whales in Australia (above).

Arrival: a humpback whale (opposite) reaches the goal of its northward migration to Alaska.

is the principal means of gathering information for cetaceans, and we know that low-frequency sound can travel oceanic distances, so could potentially be used if the whale knew how to interpret it. Recent discoveries of slowly repeated low-frequency tonal calls by large baleen whales on migration may even be their equivalent of echolocation. If so, the sounds are designed to gather information from objects very far away – conceivably sub-marine ridges or even distant shorelines.

and beach themselves again in the same spot. If they have been used to following magnetic cues successfully all their lives, they might continue to do so, especially if their echolocation signals are creating confusion by bouncing off unfamiliar shallow sea beds and beaches. It is no coincidence that mass strandings invariably involve deep-water species like sperm and pilot whales – creatures which would not normally encounter shallow water, surf, bays and beaches.

Voices in the Deep

For much the same reason that sound is used as the principal means of gaining information about a cetacean's surroundings, so it is also used as the means of communication between individuals. Water transmits sound energy so efficiently that, in theory, whales producing low-frequency sounds in certain circumstances could be heard by other whales hundreds or even thousands of miles away. We have no way of telling whether such long-range communication is used, or what function it might have, but a lot of research has been carried out on communication between cetaceans in closer contact.

Probably the best-known cetacean sound, among humans at least, is that of the song of the humpback whale. Made only by adult males, and principally during the mating season, humpback song probably has a similar function to much birdsong – that of sexual advertisement. First described by Roger Payne and Scott McVay in 1971, and the subject of study in many parts of the world since then, we now know that the song of the humpback is surprisingly complex. A typical 20-minute rendition, during which time the whale hangs motionless and head-down, comprises sequences of phrases which are repeated in the same order every time. We also know that there is a strong cultural influence in each song, showing that the whales plagiarize elements of the songs being sung around them. Furthermore, fashion in humpback song changes much like that in popular music. This year's offering differs from last year's, but maintains an unmistakable regional flavor.

The beauty and complexity of humpback whale song is apparently unique among cetaceans, but recent research on bowhead whales intriguingly suggests that they too may produce what we would term 'song', albeit less attractive to our ears. Two of the humpback's closest relatives, blue and fin whales, generally emit what to us are long and boring low-frequency calls not dissimilar to the rumbling boom of a fog horn.

Odontocete communication varies between species. Most marine dolphins use single-note whistles, the larger species producing a lower pitch and vice versa. River dolphins seem to differ from their oceanic counterparts in voice as well as appearance, however. The boto or Amazon river dolphin makes more complex multiple-note calls with significant harmonics, and vocalizes much less frequently, perhaps because it is a less social creature. Larger Odontocetes, including the sperm whale, seem to use what to our ears sound like 'clicks' not only for echolocation but also, in rhythmic patterns which have been termed 'codas', for communication. Research by Hal Whitehead and others has found that codas vary between pods, and are probably used as a means of identifying other members of the group (which usually means other family members). Killer whale pods are known to have 'dialects' of communication which distinguish them from other pods. Studies off western Canada have shown that two communities of killer whales, known as 'residents' and 'transients', speak totally different 'languages' and have almost no social interaction.

Like our own popular music, the songs of male humpback whales differ from region to region and evolve from year to year. Singers hang motionless in the water, often head-down, and croon away for 20 minutes at a time without taking a single breath.

we will find individual voice recognition to be a standard part of the Odontocete social scene, as it is in our own species.

A great deal of effort has been spent on the task of discovering what dolphins say to each other, or indeed say to us. Convinced that these enigmatic creatures with relatively large brains have a special and profound message for us, if only we could interpret it, a few people have dedicated large portions of their lives to the task. None has succeeded. The conclusion reached so far by more main-stream scientists is that dolphins do not possess a language in the sense that we understand the concept. This work, advanced and well respected though it is, still leaves the question

Killer whale dialects even distinguish social groups swimming in the same waters (above).

Vocal communication keeps schools of dolphins together (opposite).

Studies of wild cetaceans are hampered by the inability to be sure, in most cases, which animal is vocalizing, so it is difficult to know if individuals have recognizably different 'voices'. That difficulty is overcome in a captive environment, and indeed it has been discovered that several species of marine dolphins do have 'signature whistles' which distinguish one individual from every other. As research techniques continue to develop, it is likely that

of whether we even have the analytical tools to be able to understand the nuances of a communication system which may be very different from our own. Might not a creature which has adapted to an aquatic way of life over millions of years, and has developed all manner of (to us) extraordinary abilities in the process, have also evolved a means of communication which we cannot even recognize as such?

Social Behavior

Even today, after decades of research on the behavior of cetaceans both in the wild and in captivity, we know very little of social behavior in this diverse group of animals. The reasons for this paucity of knowledge are not hard to find. Land- or boat-based observers can barely see anything of these creatures in the habitat where they spend most of their time – below the water surface – and many species occur so sparsely and in such remote areas that even views at the surface are opportunistic or rare. The student of whale behavior looks enviously at the ornithologist whose study animals conduct their social interaction entirely above water and can be marked with colored leg-bands to aid individual recognition!

What *is* known is intriguing. As in so many other characteristics, cetacean social behavior is varied. At one extreme are large, solitary male sperm whales which may have almost no social interaction for months at a time. At the other are the intensely social marine dolphins which spend their lives in large, dense groups and routinely interact intensely with members of the group, which often includes many close relatives. Exciting new insights about the structure of whale and dolphin groups has come from genetic studies which can reveal the relatedness of each individual with every other in the group. Some of the most intriguing results have come from studies of pilot whales and killer whales, two closely related species which live in groups (a group of cetaceans is known as a pod). In contrast to many land mammals, in which males leave their family group at or near puberty and thereby avoid inbreeding (mating with close relatives), pilot and killer whale males usually remain in their natal group for life. Despite this, inbreeding seems to be avoided, probably by females mating with males from other groups during periods when two or more family groups temporarily merge. This arrangement results in the seemingly strange situation where a male cannot care for or defend its young. But of course this same male will be related to many of the females in the group which he does defend (mother, sisters, aunts etc), so their offspring will also be relatives sharing many of his genes and thereby worthy of his care and protection.

Perhaps the most well known cetacean social structure is that of the familiar bottlenose dolphin, which often occurs in bays and estuaries and therefore lends itself to study. Populations of this animal have been studied in countries as far apart as Australia, Scotland and the United States. Adult male bottlenose dolphins often form stable coalitions, and membership of these all-male groups can remain constant for years. As in lions, the purpose of joining an all-male group is to increase the reproductive success of the members, and close observation of bottlenose dolphin society confirms that male coalitions compete aggressively with each other for access to females – a form of gang warfare. The friendly, smiling 'Flipper' image has recently been further tarnished by the discovery of infanticide and porpoise killing in these dolphins.

The only river dolphin which has been studied in any

Groups of right whales can be very rowdy during the mating season, when several males vie with each other to inseminate fertile females. Ironically, most of the competition between bulls occurs within the body of the female. She will mate with many partners, and will be fertilized by the owner of the most vigorous sperm.

37

next supermarket up the road (or in this case the river) if they cannot get everything that they need.

What we know of baleen whale societies indicates that they have no more structure than river dolphin societies. Baleen whales often occur in loose aggregations at feeding sites or on breeding grounds, but there is no evidence of anything approaching the family groupings of marine dolphins, and even the mother/calf relationship is short lived – calves are usually weaned at 6-12 months of age. The tight groupings of humpback whales often seen by whale watchers are usually made up of males making amorous moves on a female. The competing males can become very aggressive with each other while trying to inseminate a female or prevent others doing the same, but baleen whales have no teeth with which to bite each other, so injuries are superficial.

Why this diversity in cetacean societies? The answer seems to be related to each species' food habits and vulnerability to predation. The marine dolphins, which form the largest groups, are relatively small creatures living in a world where food is patchy and unpredictable, and larger predators abound. The group can more effectively find and catch prey (which is itself usually group-forming, so there is plenty to go round) and can better defend itself against attackers like sharks. On the whole, species occurring in smaller groups are those that are less vulnerable to predators (because they have a larger body size, or there *are* no predators), and/or they hunt prey which is easier for the individual to find and catch.

Most marine dolphins (above) form large groups for safety and better feeding opportunities.

Sperm whales (opposite) form tight-knit matriarchal groups of related adult females and their offspring, much as do elephants.

detail is the boto, or Amazon river dolphin. Work carried out recently by Vera da Silva and myself in the Mamirauá reserve, Brazil, has found that the only stable relationship between individuals is that of a mother and her calf. The large aggregations of these dolphins which are sometimes found at junctions and bends of small rivers are simply caused by many dolphins being attracted to the same fish resource. I liken them to shoppers at a supermarket; they each come looking for food, mothers bringing their youngsters. The dolphins may meet relatives and acquaintances while there, but leave independently or with one or two temporary friends, often to move on to the

Interactions with Man

No account of whales, dolphins and porpoises would be complete without a mention of the greatest challenge they have faced in millions of years – having to share their world with industrialized man. Consider the changes they have encountered during the past millennium, particularly the last 100 years. Before man learned to hunt them, cetaceans were the top predators of the oceans, fearing almost no other creature and having evolved defenses against those they did. Early human hunts were small-scale, but as much as 1000 years ago open-boat whalers were demolishing populations of the right whale, and the advent of modern whaling with engine-powered vessels meant that even the fastest and largest species were vulnerable to the gun. During the twentieth century, hundreds of thousands of the 'great whales' were killed by commercial whaling, which reached every part of the globe.

Less than a hundred years ago, cetaceans could swim freely. Then man developed fishing nets and monofilament line, and everything changed. As little as a decade ago, more than 250,000 dolphins were killed each year in one fishery alone (the eastern Pacific tuna industry), and the global kill was far, far higher. Today, although the worst excesses of some notorious fisheries have been curbed, 'incidental' catches of cetaceans are much more common than all whaling and other deliberate killing combined. These deaths are not restricted to remote, high-seas locations; thousands of porpoises are killed each year both

in the North Sea and along the east coast of the U.S. and Canada. They drown in monofilament gill-nets set for bottom-dwelling fish destined for the tables of Europe and North America.

As little as 200 years ago, the oceans were relatively quiet places, providing an environment in which cetaceans evolved uses of sound both for communication and as the principal means of gathering information about their world. Then came engine-powered ships and boats, and sonar, and seismic exploration for undersea minerals. Immerse your head today in almost any coastal environment, or even in many parts of the deep ocean,

Bottlenose dolphins (above) are a welcome sight around our coasts, but are vulnerable to entanglement in fishing nets.

Worldwide, killer whales (opposite) are getting a bad reputation among fishermen for stealing fish off their lines.

The reality of whaling. A bull sperm whale fights to escape the rope anchored in its blubber by a harpoon. The whaler stands ready to fire a second harpoon that finally puts an end to the whale's struggle.

and be staggered at the amount of human-generated noise even our poor senses can detect. Then imagine what finely attuned cetacean senses are hearing. It is extraordinary to me that, as yet, we have little proven evidence that whales and dolphins are significantly affected by this man-made cacophony. However some recent strandings of beaked whales have been linked with simultaneous acoustic experimentation involving the production of high-energy sound, and this threat is being taken more seriously now than ever before.

Some two centuries ago, the ecology of the world's oceans and rivers was as much in equilibrium as any complex natural system is likely to be. Population levels of predators and prey fluctuated as they have always done. Natural disasters occurred, but they had localized effects. Climate change existed, but was slow. Then came industrialized man, with his increasing ability to over-exploit aquatic prey and cause environmental damage on a global scale, and at a rate far exceeding that which had gone before.

Today, a large proportion of the world's exploited fish stocks are heavily depleted, affecting the entire marine ecosystem and literally taking the food from the mouths of countless whales, dolphins and porpoises. Man is a new, and overwhelmingly successful, competitor for prey. Industrialization has resulted in large-scale chemical pollution reaching the oceans either directly through dumping or spillage, or indirectly through rivers and the atmosphere. More eerily, the rate at which we are burning fossil fuels is changing the Earth's climate, and at a speed which brings visible results in a decade, not a millennium. Cetaceans, like all creatures, have overcome environmental change before. But the ability of at least some species to adapt to the huge changes predicted, including the possible loss of the North Atlantic Gulf Stream and polar sea ice, is far from certain.

The treatment of no other group of wild animals has so tweaked the international public conscience, or motivated as many people to take action against perceived wrong-doers. An already complex situation is made much worse by the fact that there are no universal rights and wrongs in this argument. The planet's many peoples represent a wide variety of opinions on how cetaceans should be treated – from total protection to total exploitation. We must also remember that the nations which today see themselves in the vanguard of 'saving the whale' were among the worst offenders only two generations ago, and even now do more harm to the marine environment through pollution and exploitation of other resources than many of the nations they admonish.

The situation today is that large-scale commercial whaling has effectively stopped. A small number of nations are still hunting cetaceans but, with a few worrying exceptions (eg Dall's porpoises in the North Pacific) the operations are small by historical standards and do not realistically endanger the population being exploited. Commercial whaling may resume, but it will not match the massive levels of slaughter conducted in the twentieth century. This is because it would be more stringently regulated than before and, quite simply, today there are just not the numbers of large whales that existed before whaling began.

The ability of whale populations to recover once whaling was stopped has varied dramatically. On the one hand are species like gray and humpback whales, which reproduce quickly and in many areas are back up to original levels. On the other are blue, fin and sei whales of the Southern Ocean, and right whales of the Northern hemisphere, which remain very depleted and may never recover their earlier abundance. Although whaling is no

longer a serious threat, the accidental drowning of cetaceans in fishing gear continues almost unabated and kills far more individuals of more species in more areas. This is where the real concern is today, partly because it is mostly unreported and uncontrolled.

The good news is that man has not yet brought about the extinction of a single cetacean species, despite many decades of deliberate, almost unrestricted hunting. The bad news is that several species are genuinely close to extinction and one, the baiji or Chinese river dolphin, will soon disappear for ever – not as a result of hunting, but by accident and through negligence.

The good news. Once heavily depleted by whaling, the eastern Pacific gray whale population has fully recovered and friendly calves like this are common once more.

Cetacean Families

In the remainder of this book we will look in greater detail at individual cetacean species, grouped in taxonomic families. Fourteen such families are currently recognized, four within the baleen whales and ten among the toothed whales (including dolphins and porpoises). Each family comprises between one and 36 different, but closely related, species. For convenience, families containing a single living species have often been grouped with other similar families in the following pages (for example, the river dolphins are treated together).

Right and Gray Whales

Five species of baleen whale with a highly arched jawline are known as right whales. The name derives from early whalers who knew them as the 'right' whales to hunt because they yielded much oil and conveniently floated when dead. Three of these species, one from the North Atlantic, one from the North Pacific and a third from the Southern hemisphere, look very similar and are collectively known as black right whales. They are large, rotund whales with no dorsal fin at all and an extraordinary head shape dictated by the very long baleen (up to almost 10 ft / 3 m) with which these whales filter food. Unlike rorquals, right whales largely feed by swimming along with their mouths partly open, straining prey from water in a continuous process analogous to the way in which a trawl net works. Black right whales are also distinguished by 'callosities' on the head. These irregular patches of rough skin are naturally whitish in color, but become encrusted with communities of ectoparasites such as barnacles and lice which can give them a yellowish appearance.

The fibers of right whale baleen are the finest of any whale, and as a result these huge animals are able to make a living on the tiniest prey. Zooplankton as small as $1/8$ inch (3 mm) in length are often taken. Black right whales are migratory, traveling from high latitude feeding grounds in summer to traditional lower latitude breeding areas for the winter. This predictability has been known and exploited by humans for centuries. Right whales were the first large whales to be hunted, and the first to be almost wiped out. They are still very depleted throughout their range and, in areas such as the North Atlantic, may never recover from centuries of slaughter despite complete protection from hunting for decades. The ability to know where and when whales will turn up, and to identify individuals using the callosity pattern, has allowed scientists to study right whales in some detail. Our knowledge of these animals is therefore better than it is for many of the other great whales.

The bowhead whale is very similar to the black right whales, but is distinguishable on the basis of having a white 'chin' and no callosities on the head. The bowhead is restricted

Going down. Right whales often forage on the sea bed, and announce their intentions by lifting their tail flukes high after the last breath in a sequence. They may return to the surface 15 minutes later with tell-tale mud on their snout.

to Arctic waters, and has the ability to break a moderate thickness of ice from below if this is necessary to breathe. Perhaps the most extraordinary feature of this species is its longevity. Recent discoveries of ancient spear-points in the blubber of whales harvested in Alaska have provided proof that bowhead whales can live to well in excess of 100 years of age, making them the longest-lived of any cetacean. This longevity is matched by slow growth, delayed maturity and low reproductive rates, and is partly due to there being little or no disease within the population. The bowhead is still hunted in Alaska, but the harvest of fewer than 100 whales is thought to be sustainable because the exploited population numbers some 6000-9000 individuals. In contrast, bowhead populations in eastern Canada and Svalbard / Franz Josef Land are still very depleted from commercial whaling more than a century ago; only a few hundred remain here.

The last whale in this group, the pygmy right whale, differs from the others in several regards and is placed in a separate taxonomic sub-family – Neobalaenidae. As its name implies, this whale is smaller (up to about 21 ft / 6.5m) and, with a dorsal fin and streamlined body, its appearance is more similar to that of the rorquals. Only the strongly arched jawline marks it as a relative of the corpulent and ponderous larger right whales. Pygmy right whales have been little studied and never hunted. They are confined to mid-latitudes

The callosities on the head of this right whale (opposite) leave no doubt as to its identity. Similarly, the white crescent and black 'beads' in this photo (right) can only mean that the monstrous bulk of a bowhead whale is lurking behind this chin.

of the Southern hemisphere.

The gray whale shares characteristics of both the right whales and the rorquals, but is sufficiently different to justify being placed in its own family, Eschrichtiidae. The history of this whale can be traced back only some 100,000 years, which is very recent in evolutionary terms, so little is known of its origins. Today's gray whales are all found in the North Pacific Ocean, but there is intriguing evidence that they may have occurred in the North Atlantic until the seventeenth or even eighteenth centuries, and may then have been exterminated by whaling. The gray whale is a filter feeder with a pointed head, short and coarse baleen, and two to four short throat grooves. It is unique among all baleen whales in finding most of its food in the mud or sand of the sea bed, often in shallow coastal waters where it leaves a plume of debris in its wake. By far the majority of gray whales alive today belong to the eastern North Pacific population which summers in the very cold waters of Alaska and Siberia, then migrates along the western coast of North America down to traditional breeding lagoons in Baja California, Mexico. This stock of whales was heavily depleted by whaling in the nineteenth and twentieth centuries, but has subsequently recovered to original levels and is now a common sight during the migration periods along the western coasts of Mexico, California, Oregon and British Columbia.

This playful young gray whale shows off its
chunky foreparts and small, rounded flipper (opposite).
The baleen of gray whales (left) is often shorter on one side,
depending on whether its owner is a left- or right-flippered feeder.

Rorquals

Eight species of large, sleek filter-feeding whales are known as rorquals, varying in size from the 150 ton blue whale to the 8 ton minke whale. Most rorquals are highly migratory, moving into high latitudes in summer to take advantage of the seasonal explosion of food, then retreating to warmer tropical or sub-tropical waters in winter for mating and calving.

The blue whale was famous as an icon of the anti-whaling movement of the 1970s and 1980s because it was severely over-hunted wherever it occurred and many populations were pushed to perilously low levels. Today, after more than 30 years of protection, blue whales are making a recovery in areas where their abundance can be measured. However, they remain very rare (low thousands) in the waters around Antarctica where hundreds of thousands were removed in the early and middle decades of the twentieth century.

The situation is rather better for the other rorquals that were, or still are, subjected to whaling. Fin and sei whales were harvested in many parts of the world

including the Antarctic, and are still depleted but making a comeback. Humpback whales, being the slowest swimmers of the group and occurring in predictable areas, were especially targeted and ruthlessly depleted, but many populations (e.g. North Atlantic) are now at, or close to, original levels due to their high breeding rate. Minke whales, being relatively small, were not targeted by whalers until the industry was in decline, and as a result have not

Largest of all whales, the blue (above and opposite) was the favored prey of whalers but is now making a comeback in some areas. Blue whales often feed in coastal waters.

The minke whale (above) has a distinctive white flipper patch. The body pattern on this one is characteristic of the 'dwarf' form – here off the Great Barrier Reef.

Humpback whales (opposite) breaching in the sheltered waters of southern Alaska.

been depleted to the same extent as their larger cousins. Today, though, they are one of only two rorquals subject to whaling. Hundreds are taken annually in the Antarctic, North Atlantic and North Pacific, where their populations are strong.

The humpback whale is probably the most charismatic of all whales. Apart from its haunting song (see Voices in the Deep), this is the animal known for its extravagant breaching and lob-tailing behavior and also for our ability to recognize individuals through the unique pattern each has on the underside of its tail. This discovery was made by scientists in the 1970s, and has been used as a powerful

scientific tool ever since. Catalogs of photographs of named whales have been set up by enthusiasts for humpback populations all over the world. New photos are submitted every year, compared with the existing catalog to see if the whale is known, and added if no match is found. In this way, we know when particular females give birth (leading to estimates of breeding rate), the end-points of migration paths, and when individuals suddenly disappear from a customary feeding or breeding ground (usually at their death, providing information on mortality rates). Using mark-recapture techniques, good estimates of population size can also be made, and have recently demonstrated that North Atlantic humpbacks are more numerous than previously thought (there are currently about 10,000 in this ocean).

Some of the most remarkable discoveries to come from photo-ID work, as it has been termed, concern the migration of humpback whales. In the North Pacific, for example, humpbacks breeding as far apart as Japan, Hawaii and Mexico in the winter mix on a common feeding ground off Alaska in summer. In contrast, humpbacks in the North Atlantic breed together in small areas of the Caribbean, but then split into several widely separated feeding grounds in summer. It has recently been discovered that humpbacks feeding west of the Antarctic Peninsula make the longest known migration of any mammal, traveling up the coast of South America to breeding grounds north of the equator off Colombia.

Two other characteristics of humpback whales relate

A long, smooth back with a small dorsal fin is characteristic of all rorquals. The size and color of the body, together with the position, size and shape of the fin distinguishes this as Balaenoptera physalus – *better known as a fin whale.*

Best known of all the whales, the humpback is famous for its long flippers and knobbly head.
This youngster is taking a close look at the photographer.

Bryde's whales (above) are restricted to low latitudes and do not undertake long migrations.

Feeding as a team, humpback whales (opposite) explode through the surface, their throats bulging with tons of water.

The non-conformists of the rorquals, in that they remain in warm waters year-round, are the Bryde's whale and a closely allied species only recently recognized — Eden's whale. These mid-sized rorquals are superficially similar to the sei whale, but have two distinctive longitudinal ridges on the rostrum, the flat part of the head

The fin whale, second in size only to the blue whale, is unique among all whales in that its mandible is asymmetrically colored — grey-brown on the left and white on the right. There is no certainty about the reason for this asymmetry, but it is assumed to be used during feeding, the white skin perhaps frightening and corralling dispersed prey into a tight aggregation so the whale can engulf more per mouthful.

As with Bryde's and Eden's whales, the two minke whales, one confined to the Southern hemisphere and the other to the Northern, have only recently been recognized as separate species. Once again, genetic evidence has indicated that similar-looking animals are in fact very distinctly different. Both the Antarctic minke whale and the Northern minke whale are abundant and widely distributed. One or other species is found in every ocean of the world, and diminutive minke whales reach higher latitudes than any other rorqual. They are a common sight in the pack ice of Antarctica, and the most abundant whale in the northern reaches of the North Atlantic around the Svalbard archipelago, only 500 miles (800 km) from the North Pole.

to feeding. The first is that groups of humpbacks sometimes feed cooperatively, and with the same partners from year to year. The sight of them bursting through the surface together with mouths agape, spilling fish and water in every direction, is spectacular. The second is that humpback whales in many areas use a feeding technique called 'bubble-netting', whereby one or two whales spiral up from depth while simultaneously releasing air slowly from their blowholes. The result is a cylindrical 'net' of bubbles which concentrates prey, and the whale or whales then surge through the middle of the net with mouth agape, bursting the surface after engulfing the dense swarm of krill or fish.

Sperm Whales

Three species are known as sperm whales, though at first sight there are few similarities between *the* sperm whale on the one hand, and the relatively tiny *pygmy* and *dwarf* sperm whales on the other. This difference is such that the sperm whale is by far the largest of all the toothed whales, whereas the dwarf sperm whale is actually the smallest cetacean known as a whale. Apart from this, the head of the larger species is much larger in relation to body size (around a third of body length in adult bulls), and the dorsal fin is less distinct. The three species share the characteristics of a small, underslung lower jaw, a large melon, and tiny non-functional teeth in the upper jaw. They also have similar habitat preferences – deep, off-shore waters.

Little is known of the pygmy and dwarf sperm whales. Strandings indicate that both species occupy warm waters in all oceans, and food remains in stomachs show that they primarily eat cephalopods (squid and cuttlefish) which are captured on or close to the sea bed in continental shelf waters. Groups are usually of mixed sex and body size. In contrast, the sperm whale is better known than most whales, due largely to the fact that it has been heavily hunted worldwide for two centuries. Much of what we know about this extraordinary animal is hard to believe. Adult males are much larger than females – more than twice their weight – and spend most of their time isolated from them in higher latitudes. Females remain in warmer waters year-round, and form groups which are in effect an extended family. Males

leave these groups in adolescence to form 'bachelor' pods, becoming more isolated with age until reaching the status of a 'lone bull', when they compete for access to reproductive females. Sperm whales are probably the champion divers among all cetaceans, males able to remain submerged for well over an hour and to reach depths of more than a mile (1.5 km). They are also famous for eating giant squid which can be many meters long, though how they approach, subdue and consume such a huge animal in the dark depths is still unknown. Smaller squid and fish are more common prey, but the capture of even these very mobile animals by a massive, sluggish beast with a small mouth stretches the imagination.

A sperm whale's huge head and narrow, underslung jaw (opposite) are unique. Its tail (above) is shown above the surface only when it begins a deep dive.

The beluga is the only truly white whale. The fabled Moby Dick was but an albino sperm whale.

Beluga and Narwhal

These two small whales are the only living members of the family Monodontidae – literally 'one-tooth'. The name comes from the narwhal, one of the most bizarre of all whales, in which the male has a single modified tooth protruding through the left upper lip to form an impressive tusk. This tusk, which grows spirally and to a length of around 10 ft (3 m), is the source of the unicorn legend. Double tuskers and females with tusks are very rare. A narwhal's mouth has no obvious teeth, but teeth there are. They just remain below the gum line throughout life, apparently no longer needed by the modern narwhal.

The purpose of the narwhal's tusk has been debated for centuries, especially since it involves the owner in no small cost. Not only are the neck vertebrae fused to deal with the weight and asymmetric pull experienced when the animal swims, but potential prey have a 10 ft (3 m) warning of the approach of a predatory mouth. The answer to this riddle is probably that the tusk is a secondary sexual characteristic, much like antlers in deer. The bigger the tusk, the more impressive the animal both in attracting females and intimidating male competitors. Although tusk tips are often broken, and are sometimes found embedded in the heads of other narwhals, it is likely that the tusk is more often used as a display than as a weapon, again just like in deer.

In contrast, the beluga, the only white whale (if you discount the rare genetic variants of other species which occur both in nature and classic American literature), has a full set of

The unmistakable shape of a male narwhal, origin of the unicorn myths.

marine mammals in this region are seals, but the larger whales can dive deeper — both species commonly reach 1000 ft (300 m) and have been recorded at depths in excess of 3300 ft (1000 m) — so have sole access to the sea bed food resources in many areas. Belugas and narwhals commonly travel far from land, into heavy pack ice. One of their remarkable skills is to locate sometimes tiny areas of water in almost unbroken ice so they can breathe. They probably do this using sound.

The beluga and narwhal are both hunted today by Inuit communities, mostly for *muk-tuk* (skin), a delicacy rich in vitamins, and the narwhal tusk as a 'cash crop' to generate income. Although some of the approximately 30 different beluga populations are

Belugas are very inquisitive. Their expressive faces make them one of the most endearing of all whales. In summer (opposite) they gather at traditional sites to moult.

short, stubby teeth. Like the narwhal, its diet is principally fish which live under sea-ice for much of the year and are usually caught on or near the sea bed. Narwhals and belugas are small whales which share an exclusively Arctic range, neither living far from ice year-round. Their migrations are dictated by the seasonal ebb and flow of the ice blanket which covers high latitudes, and they have adapted to live in an environment which few competitors can tolerate. The only other fish-eating

very depleted, the species as a whole is not in danger. The narwhal has a more restricted range, with most animals in eastern Canada and Greenland. The hunts here can sometimes be heavy, but again the species as a whole is not endangered. A longer-term problem is the reduction in the extent and thickness of the Arctic ice cover. This is proceeding very rapidly due to global warming, thereby shrinking the amount of suitable habitat for these two ice-loving whales.

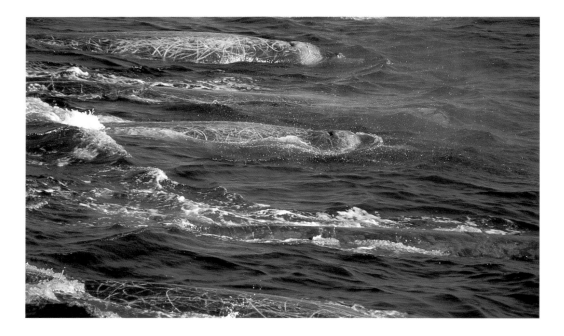

Beaked Whales

With 20 species, the beaked whale family Ziphiidae contains almost a quarter of all living cetaceans. The beaked whales range in size from around 8 ft 2 in (2.5 m) (pygmy beaked whale) to 42 ft (13 m), and all are slow-swimming, with a dorsal fin, a 'beak', few teeth (with two exceptions) and no notch in the trailing edge of the tail flukes. These are creatures of the deep ocean, rarely coming close to land and capable of long, deep dives to exploit deep-sea prey, especially squid. Beaked whales are quiet and shy, showing little of their bodies above the surface and moving in small groups. For all these reasons, even the most common species are infrequently identified at sea, while some of the rarest have never been knowingly seen. Little has been learned of their life history or migrations, or, in many species, even where they normally occur. For most, we have little or no idea of their numbers. Our lack of knowledge of these mysterious animals is exemplified by the fact that three beaked whales have only been described within the past decade.

Often the most useful diagnostic tool for distinguishing between similar-looking beaked whales is the number and position of their teeth. At sea, even this is difficult to establish, but stranded on a beach, as most closely examined beaked whales are, the head and mouth are normally visible. A complication here is that the teeth do not erupt above the gum line in the females of some species, nor in juveniles, so only adult males may be expected to have a full complement of teeth.

The largest beaked whales are the two species of *Berardius* – Baird's and Arnoux's beaked whales – both of which possess two pairs of teeth. These similar species occupy cold waters of the North Pacific and Southern hemisphere, respectively, and indeed Arnoux's beaked whales may be encountered even among Antarctic pack ice, one of the few whale species which are able to survive in this habitat. Baird's beaked whale is the only Ziphiid which is subjected to organized hunting; about 50 whales are taken annually in the western North Pacific.

Shepherd's beaked whale is the only living member of the genus *Tasmacetus*, and has more teeth than any other beaked whale, up to 90 in both the upper and lower jaws. Most records of this poorly known animal have come from New Zealand, but there is some indication that its range extends throughout the Southern Ocean. Even less is known of Longman's beaked whale, because it has only been positively identified from the bleached skulls of two long-dead stranded whales. However, recent sightings of a large unidentified beaked whale species in the Pacific and Indian Oceans may well be of this mysterious animal.

Another single-species genus is represented by Cuvier's beaked whale, *Ziphius cavirostris*. In contrast to the last species, this whale is relatively well known and occurs throughout the world in all but polar waters. Cuvier's whale has a single pair of teeth in adult males, and they are exposed even when the mouth is closed. Body size in this species is about 20-23 ft (6-7 m). Its conical head has earned it the alternative name of goose-beaked whale.

The two bottlenose whales, northern and southern, occupy similar cool-water habitat in each hemisphere and would be hard to distinguish were they ever to be seen together. Both are brown, lighter below than above, have a single pair of teeth at the tip of the lower jaw and a short, narrow beak on a bulbous head, prompting their English name. The skulls of these whales are remarkable for having two huge flanges which are thought to play a role in echolocation. Almost no light penetrates the great depths at which bottlenose whales feed, so a sensitive acoustic ability is especially vital to these animals.

The largest beaked whale genus (in fact the largest cetacean genus) is *Mesoplodon*, with 13 known living species. None of these whales grows to more than about 20 ft (6 m) in length, so they are no larger than the more familiar pilot whale. All Mesoplodon species have either one or two pairs of

teeth in the lower jaw, and Gray's beaked whale is unique in having 17-22 pairs of small teeth in the upper jaw too. The geographical range of these whales varies between species, and none occurs in the polar regions. Stejneger's, Hubbs' and the pygmy beaked whale are restricted to the North Pacific, Sowerby's to the North Atlantic, while Blainville's and the ginkgo-toothed beaked whale (so named because the teeth resemble the leaves of the Japanese ginkgo tree in shape) probably occupy warm waters in both hemispheres. Andrew's beaked whale is known only from temperate waters of the Indian and South Pacific Oceans, and True's beaked whale from both this region and the temperate North Atlantic. The straptoothed whale, which occupies cool waters of the Southern hemisphere, is an unusual beaked whale in at least two respects. It has a black and white coloration pattern which is far more complex and obvious than any other whale in this group, and adult males grow flattened teeth from the lower jaw (one on each side) which eventually encircle the narrow upper jaw and prevent the animal from opening its mouth by more than a few inches. These adornments (for these teeth have no practical function) must rank as some of the most bizarre in the entire animal kingdom.

This Cuvier's beaked whale shows why it is also known as the Goose-beaked whale. Good photos such as this are rare for any species in the group because they are not attracted to boats and remain offshore throughout life.

Marine Dolphins

The family of marine dolphins, Delphinidae, is by far the largest and most diverse taxonomic grouping of cetaceans, covering almost half of all species of whales, dolphins and porpoises known to exist today. Six of the largest animals in this family are confusingly known as whales (killer, false killer, pygmy killer, melon-headed, short-finned pilot and long-finned pilot), but genetic evidence demonstrates that they are closely allied to the 'classic' marine dolphins, so they should really be considered as large dolphins rather than small whales. The largest of these is the strikingly marked killer whale, a familiar species to millions who have visited marine parks around the world, and which is so named because it is the only species of cetacean which regularly eats warm-blooded prey. A social species like most marine dolphins, the killer whale hunts in pods and can tackle anything from the size of a blue whale down to prey as small as herring. Collectively, killer whales have the most diverse cetacean diet, but individual pods specialize on locally abundant prey and are famous for devising hunting strategies for the purpose. These range from

the rushing of a beach in Patagonia to grab a sea lion in the surf, to tipping an Antarctic ice floe with a bow-wave to dislodge a penguin or seal, to stunning shoals of fish in a Norwegian fjord with slaps of the tail.

The false killer whale and pygmy killer whale, though similar in name to the first species, share neither its appearance or diet. Both of these animals are almost black with some gray areas underneath, and both are essentially

The unmistakable white throat and eye-patch of a killer whale.

A sighting of Atlantic white-sided dolphins (opposite) in calm waters is always memorable.

the short-finned species occurs only in warm oceanic waters, and the long-finned one lives only in temperate zones. As described earlier, the long-finned pilot whale has two completely separate populations – one in the North Atlantic and the other in mid-latitudes of the Southern hemisphere. The southern animals have brighter blazes behind the eye and dorsal fin than their northern counterparts, but share the same bulbous dorsal fin set far forward on the body.

In appearance rather similar to the pilot whales, Risso's dolphin is recognized by its lack of a 'beak', its sickle-shaped dorsal fin and the tooth-scarring which becomes more extensive with age. Some adults look almost white, such is the degree to which their normal gray skin pigmentation has been replaced by lighter scar tissue. The reasons for what we presume to be a high level of biting between Risso's dolphins are not understood but this charismatic dolphin carries more scarring than almost any other cetacean.

The majority of Delphinid dolphins share a common shape and size. The best known of all must surely be the bottlenose dolphin, 'Flipper' of the television series and the species most commonly seen in aquaria worldwide. This dolphin generally prefers coastal habitats, and for this reason is commonly seen in bays, estuaries and lagoons, where groups can often be easily approached. The resident bottlenose dolphins of Monkey Mia, western Australia, are some of the best known; many have for years been coming into very shallow water for hand-feeding by tourists, and some of the dolphins are known individually by name. Fewer

fish and squid eaters. Each has a rounded head and a dorsal fin similar to most other marine dolphins. These are creatures of warm, offshore waters and they sometimes bow-ride in groups of tens or low hundreds. Similar to these animals in appearance, habitat, diet and behavior, the melon-headed whale is sometimes confused with the pygmy killer whale, but it has white lips and, despite its name, a rather less rounded head.

The long-finned pilot whale and short-finned pilot whale look almost identical, the main difference between them being flipper length and a subtle difference in the skull. They do, however, have very different habitat preferences:

The heavy dorsal fins and bulbous heads of these short-finned pilot whales separate them from all but
their long-finned cousin. Remarkably, the two species have very different habitat preferences, and almost never meet.

in number, but equally well-known, are the lone, eccentric bottlenose dolphins which live in harbors in western Europe and play with boats and swimmers. One of the most famous is 'Fungi', still alive and supporting a small local tourism industry in Dingle Harbour, Ireland, today, having arrived there in 1984. 'Fungi' is one of the most northerly bottlenose dolphins, which are found in warm and temperate latitudes and vary dramatically in size from region to region.

Bottlenose dolphins have adult body lengths of 6.5-13 ft (2-4m), weights of 220-1430 lb (100-650kg), a falcate dorsal fin and a 'beak' with 18-27 teeth in each row. The diversity of size and coloration among bottlenose dolphins across the world has generated scientific controversy about whether there is more than one species of dolphin within the genus *Tursiops*. Recent genetic evidence has confirmed this to be the case, and the Indian Ocean population is now recognized as *Tursiops aduncus*.

Looking like a miniature bottlenose dolphin, but in its own genus *Sotalia*, the tucuxi is remarkable for having distinct populations in marine waters of eastern South and Central

America and in the Amazon and Orinoco rivers. The marine form of this energetic dolphin is considerably larger than its freshwater cousin which is one of the smallest of all cetaceans, with a body length of around 5 ft (1.5m). Four other dolphins in this family are well known for their liking of freshwater or estuarine habitats — the three humpback dolphins of the genus *Sousa* and the Irrawaddy dolphin. The latter has superficial similarities to the beluga whale, but is

The characteristic upright dorsal fin and scarred body of a Risso's dolphin.

A school of bottlenose dolphins (opposite) bow-riding in clear water.

71

diminutive body seemingly so vulnerable in the tempestuous Southern Ocean where it occurs.

Described by the famous British taxonomist F.C. Fraser as recently as 1956 on the basis of a skeleton collected in Sarawak, the external appearance of Fraser's dolphin, *Lagenodelphis hosei* was not known until 1971, when specimens were collected from several tropical localities at almost the same time. This species has now been seen and photographed many times on the high seas, its preferred habitat, but it remains one of the least known of all dolphins. Adult Fraser's dolphins are strikingly marked; a broad, dark stripe runs along the side from the face to around the vent, giving it a masked appearance. This, combined with its short beak and small, upright, triangular fin, distinguishes Fraser's dolphin from all other species, so it is all the more remarkable that such a distinctive animal could have escaped detection for so long.

A distinctive grouping of four very small dolphins is represented by the genus *Cephalorhynchus*: Heaviside's, Chilean, Hector's and Commerson's dolphins. These charming animals all prefer coastal habitats, and as a result have all been subjected to accidental entrapment in fishing gear. Hector's dolphin, restricted to New Zealand, is particularly vulnerable to monofilament fishing nets, and net-free reserves have been established to help protect this most attractive species from further harm. The tiny Commerson's dolphin, with its distinct black-and-white markings, is a familiar resident of coastlines and harbors of the southern tip of South America and the Falkland Islands.

Arguably the most beautiful of all dolphins, Hector's dolphin is confined to coastal waters of New Zealand.

Atlantic spotted dolphins (opposite) only gain their characteristic spots in adulthood.

genetically very much a dolphin.

Six closely related marine dolphins of the 'classic' shape form the genus *Lagenorhynchus*. Two of these occur in the North Atlantic (white-beaked and Atlantic white-sided dolphins), one in the North Pacific (Pacific white-sided dolphin), and three in cooler waters of the Southern hemisphere (Peale's, hourglass and dusky dolphins). These are some of the most strikingly marked of all cetaceans. A school of them encountered at sea, especially when they leap out of the waves to follow a vessel in rough weather, provides an unforgettable experience. The handsome hourglass dolphin is a particular favorite of mine, its

Here, groups can sometimes be seen surfing over and over again in the breakers, a behavior which can surely only be interpreted as play.

The genus *Lissodelphis* embraces just two species of dolphin, but what dolphins they are! The northern and southern right whale dolphins are named for their lack of a dorsal fin and, though they now occupy widely separated ranges and have different color patterns, they are so similar in form that one population must surely have evolved from an offshoot of the other. These slim, rapidly swimming animals are often seen 'porpoising' in large schools of hundreds or even thousands of individuals, the sea almost boiling with their splashes.

Arguably the best-known dolphins of the tropics belong to the genus *Stenella*. Five species are represented here, three with continuous low-latitude distributions (striped, spinner and pan-tropical spotted dolphins), and two found only in the Atlantic (clymene and Atlantic spotted dolphins). The spinner dolphin is renowned as an aerial acrobat. They launch themselves like rockets, then spin on their long axis and drop to the water in an ungainly splash. There are many different populations of this species around the world, some even with their dorsal fins shaped as though they have been 'put on the wrong way round', but as yet all are considered to be of the same species. The clymene dolphin, also known as the short-snouted spinner

Spinner dolphins (opposite).
The delicate patterning of a Commerson's dolphin (right)
in the coastal waters of the Falkland Islands.

75

dolphin, is similar but rather less acrobatic. The two spotted dolphins are named for the body patterning of adults, and both species are commonly seen at close quarters because they love to ride the bows of yachts and ships. This is also true of the striped dolphin, which has a distinctive dark stripe leading back from the eye, separating the light-colored belly from gray sides and a darker bluish-gray dorsal surface.

Until recently thought to be a single species, two distinct populations of the common dolphin *Delphinus delphis* have now been attributed the status of separate species – the long-snouted common dolphin *D. capensis*, and the Arabian common dolphin *D. tropicalis*. The genus is restricted to tropical to warm-temperate waters of both hemispheres, and common dolphins are recognizable by the beautiful 'hour-glass' pattern on their sides. These graceful dolphins love to bow-ride, and are familiar companions to yachtsmen throughout much of the world. Sadly, they often fall victim to entanglement in fishing gear, and many strandings in southern Ireland, south-west Britain and western France are known to be caused by fishermen discarding dolphins which have drowned in their nets.

The rough-toothed dolphin is a tropical species with an unusual conical head due to the lack of an apex on the melon. The name derives from wrinkles on the enamel of the teeth, a characteristic that it shares with no other cetacean.

A small group of spotted dolphins (left) dive with a new supply of oxygen. Common dolphins (right) are among the most playful of all cetaceans. These are wave-riding.

Porpoises

Six of the smallest cetaceans, with a maximum length of 7 ft 2 in (2.2 m), are known as porpoises. They differ from all others in having teeth with a cutting edge, and they share the characteristics of having no beak, small flippers, notched tail flukes and (with one exception) a well-defined dorsal fin. The odd one out in this regard is the aptly named finless porpoise, which has no more than a small ridge along its back. Dall's porpoise stands out as being different from the other porpoises in several regards, and is placed in its own genus *Phocoenoides*. This is a very stocky animal with a markedly 'deeper' profile, especially behind the triangular dorsal fin, reflecting a powerful physique which enables this animal to swim very fast. Indeed, Dall's porpoise is the only species in this group which does move rapidly at the surface, and it is easily recognized by the 'rooster tail' water splash which it creates when traveling at speed.

Four of the porpoises (harbor, Burmeister's, finless and the vaquita) are essentially coastal animals. Dall's porpoise is the only one commonly seen in deep offshore waters, but the mysterious spectacled porpoise is probably also a creature of the deep ocean. So few records of this porpoise exist that at present all we can say is that it is probably restricted to cool waters of the Southern hemisphere.

The geographical range and abundance of porpoises

The dashing form of a Dall's porpoise breaks
the surface momentarily for a quick gasp of air.

varies dramatically. By far the most widely spread is the harbor porpoise which occurs along the coasts of the North Atlantic and North Pacific Oceans, and must number in the hundreds of thousands at least. Dall's porpoise is found right across the North Pacific, and has a population in the low millions. In contrast, the vaquita is restricted to the very northern end of the Gulf of California and has a total population of less than a thousand. The finless porpoise has populations in both marine and freshwaters, some animals living more than 600 mi (1000 km) from the sea in the Yangtze river of China.

The shallow-water, coastal habitat of most porpoises renders them particularly vulnerable to entrapment in fishing gear, and all species except the rare spectacled porpoise are known to suffer high levels of mortality from this cause. The vaquita, especially, has been pushed to critically low numbers because of drownings in gillnets. The only realistic chance for its survival would be for the removal of these nets from its range but this is proving to be a politically divisive issue.

Recent research in eastern Canada by Andrew Read and colleagues has greatly enhanced our understanding of the harbor porpoise, as a result of which this is now the best-known animal of the group. In this population, porpoises live in the fast lane, reaching reproductive age at only three to four years, then producing offspring every year until dying at an average age of less than ten years. They can dive to more than 650 ft (200 m), remarkably deep for such a small animal, and probably find most of their fish prey on or close

to the sea bed. Radio-tracking here and in European waters has shown that harbor porpoises often move seasonally, but do not undertake fixed migrations as seen in many baleen whales, for example.

The last of this family is Burmeister's porpoise, which occurs in the coastal waters of southern South America. Little is known of this unassuming dark-colored animal, but its large geographical spread and the numbers killed accidentally or deliberately, especially off Peru, suggest that it is relatively numerous. Burmeister's porpoise has a low, rounded dorsal fin situated well back on the body, and is unlikely to be confused with any other cetacean in its range.

Found along coasts throughout much of the temperate Northern hemisphere, the diminutive harbor porpoise is one of the world's most widespread and best-known cetaceans.

The striking juxtaposition of pink dolphin and lush vegetation can lead to only one conclusion – this is the Amazon,
and this strange creature is a boto, or Amazon river dolphin.

River Dolphins

The long-established name 'river dolphin' is confusing, because not all river dolphins live in rivers, and some dolphins which live in rivers are not called river dolphins! The reason for this anomaly is that the term is used in a taxonomic sense to cover a group of similar species, all but one of which live exclusively in rivers. The other cetaceans which occur in rivers (e.g. the finless porpoise and tucuxi) all have populations living in marine waters.

The question of how closely related are the river dolphins has occupied taxonomists for more than a century. They have obvious similarities which separate them from the marine dolphin family Delphinidae, but the question remains as to how a common ancestor could have founded distinct populations as far apart as Asia and South America, yet now be absent from the oceans. The fossil record is inconclusive on this point, but the consensus today is that many of the similarities are the result of convergent evolution rather than a (geologically) recent common ancestor. In other words, today's river dolphins look like each other because they have independently adapted to a similar habitat, rather than because they share the same ancestry.

Four species of river dolphin are recognized – the boto, or Amazon river dolphin, in the Amazon and Orinoco basins of South America; the Indian river dolphin in the Indus and Ganges rivers of the Indian sub-continent; the baiji or Chinese river dolphin in the Yangtze, and the La Plata river dolphin or franciscana (the odd one out) occupying

Sharing the same home as true river dolphins, tucuxis can be distinguished by their small size and upright dorsal fins.

coastal marine waters of eastern South America.

The characteristics that collectively discriminate river dolphins from all other cetaceans are a very flexible body, wide paddle-like flippers, a forceps-like 'beak' with dozens of sharp teeth, and reduced vision. The Indian river dolphin, with separate populations in the Indus and Ganges rivers, is arguably the most specialized of the group. It is effectively blind because it no longer has a crystalline lens in its eyes, sight being of little value in the turbid waters in which it lives. The loss of sight has been compensated for by development of particularly good acoustic acuity, and apparently sensitive touch. This animal swims on its side much of the time, sweeping the area in front of it acoustically by moving the head, while at the same time touching the bottom with one flipper. The Indus race of this dolphin is especially heavily depleted, primarily because the level of abstraction for agricultural irrigation schemes is such that the river almost runs dry in places.

The boto is also aptly known as the pink dolphin. Large males, in particular, are a uniform bright pink, the effect being rather spoiled by scars and wounds that are probably sustained in fights with other males. This dolphin has adapted to the cyclical flooding of the Amazon, and is comfortable swimming among the contorted roots and branches of the flooded forest, twisting and turning in pursuit of the rich fish life found here. The boto has a jaw and teeth able to crush armoured catfish and even turtles; it probably eats more species of prey than any other cetacean. The boto is certainly the most abundant of the river dolphins, partly because of its enormous geographical range, and partly because waterways in the Amazon and Orinoco river basins where it lives have not been subject to the scale of modification and exploitation which has so damaged the main rivers in Asia.

Uniquely endowed with a long, thin beak containing more than 200 tiny teeth, the secretive La Plata river dolphin, or franciscana, is sadly more often seen dead than alive because it is often the victim of entanglement in fishing nets. It occurs in estuaries and along the coasts of Argentina, Uruguay and southern Brazil. Although sharing many of the specialized physical characteristics of its closest relatives which all live in freshwater, strangely the franciscana does not occur in rivers.

The last animal in this group to consider, indeed the species which completes our look at all cetaceans alive today, also happens to be the rarest of them all – the Chinese river dolphin, or baiji. The total population of this poorly known creature is probably fewer than 100. Its demise is due to the intense human use of the Yangtze river, the only place where it lives. Firm political action could potentially save this dolphin, but there is no sign of any such help arriving in time and this will almost certainly be the first cetacean to be brought to extinction by man. More endangered by far than any whale, this diminutive animal is being allowed to slip away with hardly a voice raised in dissent, its survival incompatible with a burgeoning and fast-developing human population on the banks of this mighty river.

The flexible body, large flippers and long beak of the boto allow it to move among the tortuous roots and tangled branches of the flooded forest in search of prey. These areas are so rich in number and diversity of fish that they can sustain uniquely high densities of dolphins.

Epilogue

During many years of studying whales, dolphins and porpoises in far-flung parts of the planet I have spent countless hours in, on and beside the water getting close to them. To do the job effectively, you can't be gasping at every whale blow, each close encounter, but many exceptional days do remain in the mind. The image of my first humpback whale off Iceland is indelible, for example, as is the tantalizing glimpse of a right whale near South Georgia from a navy helicopter, and the simple beauty of common dolphins bow-riding in gin-clear water near the Great Barrier Reef. But it isn't always so pleasant. I also recall days of feeling like death due to seasickness, being frozen to death watching for belugas in the High Arctic, and being bored to death scanning mile upon mile of empty sea from the exquisitely uncomfortable cross-trees of a yacht mast. We cetacean biologists have a hard life, we really do.

Among the memories, a few very special moments stand out for their poignancy, for representing a rich mixture of visual experience, enhanced understanding and thoughtful reflection. I would like to conclude by sharing two such days with you, because they encapsulate much of the mystery and power of cetaceans, and the ease with which they can overcome the supposedly objective, emotionally detached perspective of this particular scientist, at least.

The first takes us to the River Amazon in Brazil. This is home to the boto, the pink dolphin which, in contrast to its

equivalent in the Yangtze, is thankfully still numerous. I'm paddling a dug-out canoe in a channel as wide as a city street, with dense rainforest pressing close on all sides. The water is thick with sediment from the Andes, and has the look and transparency of milky coffee. I'm quietly following a mother boto and her calf, hoping to be sufficiently silent that the dolphins are not disturbed by my presence. Even the drips off the end of the paddle risk giving the game away. It slowly dawns on me that some bits of flotsam ahead are in fact the crude floats of a fisherman's net, and that the net is apparently completely blocking the channel. Knowing that it is likely to be of thin, transparent nylon line and of large

The well-padded beluga (above) is much better adapted to the Arctic than a mere whale biologist.

Humpback whales (opposite).

my stomach is in knots and I plead with the fisherman to pull up the net. Then, with barely a ripple, the mother and calf surface on the far side with explosive puffs of exhalation, and continue serenely on their way.

The fisherman laughs at my anxiety and starts to lift the net because he says that there must be a hole through which the dolphins passed; a hole which they could not have made because the floats didn't even tremble. Sure enough, he does find a hole, barely large enough for a dolphin to pass through, but I can hardly believe the implications of what I've just seen (and, incidentally, what I've seen many times since). In water of near-zero visibility, these dolphins must have encountered this wall of net with no warning and then, without daring to touch it, searched for some irregularity that might allow passage through. Given the transparency of the fine line and the impossibility of seeing the bottom of a cup of milky coffee, this was an incredible feat, and must surely have been carried out using echolocation rather than vision. I had of course read much about cetacean acoustics, and how sensitive they can be, but these two anxious minutes in the rainforest of Brazil gave a better understanding of the exquisite acoustic skills of dolphins than could be gained from any textbook. Here, too, was a demonstration of how a cetacean can thrive in a habitat so very different to the open, marine environment occupied by most species. With acoustic acuity this good, no wonder that the submerged, tangled roots and branches of the flooded forest hold no fear for the boto.

The second occasion could hardly have been more

mesh, I'm immediately concerned that the dolphins will become entangled in the net and drown. The agitated look of the fisherman I've just spotted near the bank in a similar dug-out to my own suggests that he, too, sees trouble ahead.

The dolphins surface very briefly about a stone's throw short of the net, then disappear. I'm praying that they will notice the obstacle and make a U-turn, but fear that the floats will suddenly disappear, and the water erupt, as the botos entangle and spin. Twenty seconds pass; thirty, forty. The water remains unruffled. A full minute, and still nothing – surely by now the tiny calf must have become enmeshed and prevented from surfacing to breathe. After two minutes

different. Another day at the office, but this time some thirty miles off the Arctic coast of western Greenland, and now in a Zodiac inflatable. Today I'm big-game hunting, *really* big-game hunting, because the target is a blue whale. I'm feeling rather puny and vulnerable, bouncing from wave to wave at break-neck speed in this little rubber boat, knowing that there's a 100-ton female and her 10-ton calf somewhere beneath me. After a cat and mouse game, in which I'm unsure who is the mouse, we finally achieve our objective. The water surface not 15 ft (5 m) away bulges and smoothes before a truly gargantuan head emerges and the three of us aboard instinctively brace ourselves for the thunderous blow which will inevitably follow. After the immediate inhalation, the blowholes disappear and we see the neck region, the back, more back, the dorsal fin and finally the tail flukes as the whale completes its breathing roll. The whole process takes five seconds, during which *my* heart and breathing stop; somehow I've never quite got used to being so very close to such an awesome animal. We take our tiny sliver of skin for genetic analysis and leave the whales to continue their day, gorging on the pink swarms of krill in the area. The tissue will help reveal the relationship between blue whales here and elsewhere in the North Atlantic, and also how many blue whales there are in this ocean, some 40 years after this species was given immunity from whaling.

That occasion has remained vividly in my mind for

The explosive blow of a blue whale (right).
Common dolphin at speed (opposite).

several reasons, not least of which was the realization of how the fate of the blue whales hunted on this day was in such contrast to their counterparts half a century earlier. The calf we saw would likely die of natural causes one day far in the future – a fate not accorded many during the short, sharp period of whaling. Another thought was how, despite everything man has thrown at these creatures, there are still blue whales around to produce such huge babies. To be sure, they are still rare, but here was proof of the resilience of whales; given half a chance they will remain an important and valuable part of our planet's diverse fauna for a long time to come.

A lesson to be learned from those whales is that man has the power both to destroy cetaceans and, if he wishes, to allow them to survive and even flourish. Ignorance and the blind pursuit of wealth nearly brought about the demise of several whales during the whaling era, and it is immensely sad that the same vices are today destroying other cetacean species, albeit in less publicized and dramatic ways. Despite himself, man has not yet managed to kill off an entire species of whale, dolphin or porpoise, and we can all help to create the will to prevent him doing so in the future. This world would be so much poorer without them.

Grace and elegance – a spinner
dolphin bow-rides in the eastern Pacific.
Thankfully, not a farewell. Humpback whale populations (opposite)
survived remorseless whaling pressures and are today recovered or
recovering. With today's better understanding of cetaceans, there is
no excuse for any to face similar threats at the hands of man.

LATIN NAME	COMMON NAME	WHERE FOUND
ORDER CETACEA		
SUBORDER MYSTICETI		
FAMILY BALAENIDAE	**RIGHT WHALES**	
Eubalaena glacialis	North Atlantic right whale	N. Atlantic Ocean
Eubalaena japonica	North Pacific right whale	N. Pacific Ocean
Eubalaena australis	Southern right whale	Southern hemisphere; temperate & subpolar zones
Balaena mysticetus	Bowhead whale	Arctic region
FAMILY NEOBALAENIDAE	**PYGMY RIGHT WHALE**	
Caperea marginata	Pygmy right whale	Southern hemisphere; temperate zones
FAMILY ESCHRICHTIIDAE	**GRAY WHALE**	
Eschrichtius robustus	Gray whale	N. Pacific Ocean, mostly coastal
FAMILY BALAENOPTERIDAE	**RORQUALS**	
Megaptera novaeangliae	Humpback whale	All oceans
Balaenoptera acutorostrata	Northern minke whale	Northern hemisphere
Balaenoptera bonaerensis	Antarctic minke whale	Southern hemisphere
Balaenoptera edeni	Eden's whale	Low latitudes
Balaenoptera brydei	Bryde's whale	
Balaenoptera borealis	Sei whale	All oceans
Balaenoptera physalus	Fin whale	All oceans & Mediterranean Sea
Balaenoptera musculus	Blue whale	All oceans
SUBORDER ODONTOCETI		
FAMILY PHYSETERIDAE	**SPERM WHALE**	
Physeter macrocephalus	Sperm whale	All oceans & Mediterranean Sea

LATIN NAME	COMMON NAME	WHERE FOUND
FAMILY KOGIIDAE	**PYGMY SPERM WHALES**	
Kogia breviceps	Pygmy sperm whale	Warm waters worldwide
Kogia sima	Dwarf sperm whale	Warm waters worldwide
FAMILY ZIPHIIDAE	**BEAKED WHALES**	
Ziphius cavirostris	Cuvier's beaked whale	All but polar waters worldwide. Offshore
Berardius arnuxii	Arnoux's beaked whale	Southern Ocean
Berardius bairdii	Baird's beaked whale	N. Pacific Ocean, offshore. Temperate zone
Tasmacetus sheperdii	Shepherd's beaked whale	Southern hemisphere, cold temperate. Offshore
Indopacetus pacificus	Longman's beaked whale	Probably tropical Indian & Pacific Oceans
Hyperoodon ampullatus	Northern bottlenose whale	Cold temperate & sub-polar North Atlantic, offshore
Hyperoodon planifrons	Southern bottlenose whale	Southern Ocean
Mesoplodon hectori	Hector's beaked whale	Southern hemisphere temperate zone
Mesoplodon mirus	True's beaked whale	N. Atlantic & Indian Oceans, temperate zones
Mesoplodon europaeus	Gervais' beaked whale	Atlantic Ocean, tropical to warm temperate zones
Mesoplodon bidens	Sowerby's beaked whale	N. Atlantic Ocean offshore; temperate zones
Mesoplodon grayi	Gray's beaked whale	Southern hemisphere, temperate zones
Mesoplodon peruvianus	Pygmy beaked whale	Eastern Tropical Pacific Ocean
Mesoplodon bowdoini	Andrew's beaked whale	Probably temperate zones of Southern hemisphere
Mesoplodon traversii	Spade-toothed whale	South Pacific Ocean
Mesoplodon carlhubbsi	Hubbs' beaked whale	North Pacific Ocean; temperate zones
Mesoplodon ginkgodens	Ginkgo-toothed whale	Indian & Pacific Oceans, tropical to warm temperate zones
Mesoplodon stejnegeri	Stejneger's beaked whale	N. Pacific Ocean; cold temperate to subarctic zones
Mesoplodon layardii	Strap-toothed whale	Southern Ocean; cold temperate zone
Mesoplodon densirostris	Blainville's beaked whale	Worldwide in tropical to cold temperate zones. Offshore
Mesoplodon perrinii	Perrin's beaked whale	N. Pacific Ocean; temperate zone
FAMILY PLATANISTIDAE	**INDIAN RIVER DOLPHIN**	
Platanista gangetica	Indian river dolphin, susu, bhulan	Indus, Ganges & Brahmaputra river systems, Asia

LATIN NAME	COMMON NAME	WHERE FOUND
FAMILY INIIDAE	**AMAZON RIVER DOLPHIN**	
Inia geoffrensis	Boto, Amazon river dolphin	Amazon & Orinoco rivers
FAMILY LIPOTIDAE	**CHINESE RIVER DOLPHIN**	
Lipotes vexillifer	Baiji, Chinese river dolphin	Yangtze river
FAMILY PONTOPORIIDAE	**LA PLATA DOLPHIN**	
Pontoporia blainvillei	Franciscana, La Plata river dolphin	Coast of S.E. South America
FAMILY MONODONTIDAE	**BELUGA AND NARWHAL**	
Delphinapterus leucas	Beluga, white whale	Circumpolar Arctic
Monodon monoceros	Narwhal	Arctic
FAMILY DELPHINIDAE	**DOLPHINS**	
Cephalorhynchus commersonii	Commerson's dolphin	Southeast S. America & Kerguelen Isles, coastal
Cephalorhynchus eutropia	Chilean dolphin, black dolphin	Western coast of southern S. America
Cephalorhynchus heavisidii	Heaviside's dolphin	Western coast of Southern Africa, coastal
Cephalorhynchus hectori	Hector's dolphin	New Zealand, coastal
Steno bredanensis	Rough-toothed dolphin	Warm waters worldwide
Sousa teuszii	Atlantic humpback dolphin	Coast of tropical W. Africa
Sousa plumbea	Indian humpback dolphin	Coasts of Indian Ocean
Sousa chinensis	Pacific humpback dolphin, Chinese white dolphin	Coasts of S.E. Asia & Northern Australia
Sotalia fluviatilis	Tucuxi	Atlantic coast & main rivers of tropical S. & central America
Tursiops truncatus	Bottlenose dolphin	Pacific & Atlantic Oceans in all but coldest waters. Mostly coastal
Tursiops aduncus	Indian Ocean bottlenose dolphin	Indian Ocean , mostly coastal
Stenella attenuata	Pantropical spotted dolphin	Warm waters worldwide
Stenella frontalis	Atlantic spotted dolphin	Warm waters of Atlantic Ocean
Stenella longirostris	Spinner dolphin	Tropics & sub-tropics
Stenella clymene	Clymene dolphin, short-snouted spinner dolphin	Tropics & sub-tropics of Atlantic Ocean. Deep water
Stenella coeruleoalba	Striped dolphin	Warm waters worldwide
Delphinus delphis	Common dolphin, saddleback dolphin	Tropical to warm temperate waters worldwide

LATIN NAME	COMMON NAME	WHERE FOUND
Delphinus capensis	Long-beaked common dolphin	Nearshore tropical and warm temperate waters
Delphinus tropicalis	Arabian common dolphin	N. Indian Ocean and S.E. Asia
Lagenodelphis hosei	Fraser's dolphin	Pantropical, offshore
Lagenorhynchus albirostris	White-beaked dolphin	N. Atlantic shelf waters, cold temperate zone
Lagenorhynchus acutus	Atlantic white-sided dolphin	N. Atlantic shelf waters, cold temperate zone
Lagenorhynchus obliquidens	Pacific white-sided dolphin	N. Pacific Ocean, temperate zone
Lagenorhynchus obscurus	Dusky dolphin	Cool waters of Southern hemisphere. Mostly coastal
Lagenorhynchus australis	Peale's dolphin	Southern tip of S. America & Falklands. Coastal
Lagenorhynchus cruciger	Cruciger's dolphin, hour-glass dolphin	Southern Ocean, offshore
Lissodelphis borealis	Northern right whale dolphin	N. Pacific Ocean, offshore. Temperate zone
Lissodelphis peronii	Southern right whale dolphin	Southern Ocean, temperate zone
Grampus griseus	Risso's dolphin	Tropical to temperate zones, worldwide
Peponocephala electra	Melon-headed whale	Warm waters worldwide
Feresa attenuata	Pygmy killer whale	Warm waters worldwide
Pseudorca crassidens	False killer whale	Warm waters worldwide
Orcinus orca	Killer whale	Worldwide
Globicephala melas	Long-finned pilot whale	Cool waters of N. Atlantic & Southern hemisphere
Globicephala macrorhynchus	Short-finned pilot whale	Warm waters worldwide
Orcaella brevirostris	Irrawaddy dolphin, pesut	Southeast Asia & N. Australia, coastal. Some rivers
FAMILY PHOCOENIDAE	PORPOISES	
Neophocaena phocaenoides	Finless porpoise	Southeast Asia, coastal and some rivers
Phocoena phocoena	Harbor porpoise, common porpoise	N. Atlantic & N. Pacific Oceans, coastal. Temperate zones
Phocoena sinus	Vaquita	Northern tip of Gulf of California, Mexico
Phocoena spinipinnis	Burmeister's porpoise, black porpoise	Southern South America, coastal
Phocoena dioptrica	Spectacled porpoise	Southern Ocean, offshore
Phocoenoides dalli	Dall's porpoise	North Pacific Ocean, cold temperate zone

Index

Recommended Reading

Marine Mammal Biology: an evolutionary approach. (Ed. A. Rus Hoelzel) Blackwell Publishing.
Sea Mammals of the World. Randall Reeves, Brent Stewart, Phillip Clapham, James Powell and Pieter Folkens. A & C Black, London.